AEI Legislative Analyses

Balanced analyses of current proposals before the Congress, prepared with the help of specialists in law, economics, and government

Proposals to Modify the Taxation of U.S. Citizens Working Abroad

1981

97th Congress
1st Session

American Enterprise Institute
for Public Policy Research
Washington and London

ISBN 0-8447-0242-0
Legislative Analysis No. 27, 97th Congress
July 1981

Contents

1 Introduction 1

2 Background 2
- Principles Influencing Tax Policy Generally .... '2
- U.S. Income Tax Treatment Compared with That of Other Countries 3
- Prior U.S. Law 7
- Current Law 8
- U.S. Citizens Potentially Affected 10

3 Principal Legislative Proposals 11

4 Issues and Arguments 22
- Effect on International Trade Objectives 22
- Cost of Tax Policy Options 28
- Fairness 29

Notes to Text 36

1

Introduction

Various policy objectives that cannot all be satisfied at the same time have influenced the federal tax treatment of income of U.S. citizens who live and work abroad. Thus, not surprisingly, none of the major alternatives tried heretofore has commanded unanimous support.

Continued discontent with the federal tax treatment of foreign-earned income of U.S. citizens who live and work abroad has caused a reappraisal of the current law. Numerous proposals have been advanced for dealing with the issues. This legislative analysis will examine the background of the existing law, its current thrust, the principal options for changing the law, and the arguments for and against the various proposals.

This analysis will deal solely with the tax treatment of foreign income earned by U.S. citizens in the private sector. Thus, the tax treatment of military personnel and civilian employees of the federal government is outside the scope of this analysis.

2

BACKGROUND

PRINCIPLES INFLUENCING TAX POLICY GENERALLY

Participants in the debate over the taxation of the foreign-earned income of U.S. citizens living and working abroad rely on various principles to justify their positions as to the direction tax policy should take. Many proponents of current proposals to reform the law are concerned primarily with our penetration of foreign markets—export and foreign trade objectives. Some participants in the debate prefer a policy of tax neutrality, that is, a policy that will neither encourage nor discourage U.S. citizens to live and work abroad and that will neither encourage nor discourage employers in deciding whether to hire Americans or workers of other nationalities for their overseas operations.

Some participants in the debate advocate policies that serve the objectives of "tax equity," either horizontal equity or vertical equity. Policies promoting horizontal equity would promote equal tax treatment for those of equal income and circumstances, including those with families of equal size. Policies promoting vertical equity would promote the greater taxation of those with greater ability to pay—the so-called progressive taxation. Some who have entered the debate consider important other notions of fairness, such as the need to offset the extra costs borne by some U.S. workers overseas, the hardships suffered by workers in some locations abroad, and the difficulties of providing living conditions comparable to those enjoyed in the United States.

Some participants in the debate are concerned with revenue losses should U.S. citizens residing abroad be taxed less heavily. Others argue that the benefit theory of taxation should prevail: those living and working overseas should pay either no U.S. taxes or very low taxes, for they receive essentially no benefits from U.S. expenditure of tax funds.

The application of some of the foregoing principles is not as simple as their statement would indicate. Horizontal equity can mean one thing if the tax treatment of U.S. citizens working in a particular country abroad is compared with that of citizens working in the United States, but quite a different thing if the tax treatment of U.S. citizens working in a country is compared with that of natives of that country or with expatriates of other nations working from country to country and from circumstance to circumstance. Thus, the factual setting for the debate is anything but simple, and the policy directions advocated have different consequences for different persons and in different circumstances and countries.

U.S. Income Tax Treatment Compared with That of Other Countries

Comparison of U.S. tax treatment with that afforded by other nations is important to the debate over U.S. tax policy for a variety of reasons. How the United States and the host country respectively tax the income of a worker affects the ability of U.S. firms to compete in the world market and has a major bearing on the fairness concerns of the worker and tax equity concerns of tax authorities. Whether the host country taxes income at a higher or lower marginal tax rate than that at which the United States taxes income determines whether the foreign tax credit substantially benefits workers and whether an exclusion from taxes of all or some part of foreign-earned income might encourage U.S. citizens to work in that country.

Most countries impose a tax on nonresidents' income that is earned within the host country and on their residents' worldwide income. This practice is true of major trade competitors of the United States such as Canada, the Federal Republic of Germany, France, Japan, and the United Kingdom. Most countries, however, do not impose taxes on the foreign-source income of their nonresident citizens.[1] A few countries, such as Saudi Arabia, do not impose an income tax on U.S. citizens who work there. The United States, on the other hand, imposes taxes on a citizenship basis; that is, it taxes the worldwide income of its citizens, whether the citizens reside in the United States or elsewhere. The United States is alone among the major industrialized nations in taxing foreign-source income on a citizenship basis.[2] Table 1 illustrates how the U.S. tax treatment of its citizens residing and working abroad compares with that of certain other countries whose citizens reside and work abroad.

The U.S. tax law does provide a dollar-for-dollar tax credit for the amount of income taxes paid by a U.S. citizen to the host country where he works, but the credit may not exceed the rate of the U.S. tax applicable to the income on which the foreign tax was paid.[3] The tax credit recognizes the tax primacy of the country in which the income is earned, and the credit is granted to prevent the hardship of double taxation of the same income by two governments.[4] If a U.S. citizen resides and works in a country having a higher income tax rate than that of the United States, the credit will offset or cancel out U.S. taxes on income earned in that country; but, of course, the worker will pay more taxes than if the United States were the only taxing jurisdiction. If the host country has a lower income tax rate than the United States, the worker will pay that tax and enough more to the United States so the combined tax rate on that income equals the rate he or she would pay the United States. If the host country has no income tax, the worker simply pays the required U.S. tax. Table 2 lists countries in which the foreign tax

TABLE 1

Comparison of Tax Policies for Overseas Employees

Country	*Tax on Salary*	*Tax on Incentives/ Bonuses*	*Tax on Benefits (retirement, health, insurance, etc.)*	*Tax on Cost-of-Living Allowances*	*Tax on Additional Income Earned Out of Home Country*	*Government Subsidies (to individuals)*
United States	Yes[a]	Yes	Yes[b]	Yes	Yes	No
Japan	No	No	No	No	No[c]	Yes
Italy	No[d]	No	No	No[e]	Complex formulas to discourage foreign investments.	Government-owned companies.
France	No[f,g]	No	No	No	Complex formulas.	Government-owned companies.

[a] $20,000 exclusion under section 911 for those living in qualified camps.

[b] Certain deductions permitted under complex section 913 tests.

[c] Rental, interest, etc., on off-shore investments totally exempt from taxation during nonresidence status only.

[d] Complex nonresidency requirements.

[e] Limitation placed on daily expenses for home leave and rest and recreation.

[f] Assumes accompanied tour; rules for dual residency (unaccompanied) very complex.

[g] Recent government policy is aimed at encouraging more French engineers to accept overseas work.

Korea	No[h]	No	No	No	No	Yes
Germany	No[i]	No[j]	No	No[k]	Some limitations; generally liberal.	Few
Canada	No[l]	No	No	No	No	No
Sweden	No[m]	No	No	No	No	Few
United Kingdom	No	No	No[n]	No[o]	Complex requirements.	Few

[h] Most liberal policies with respect to individuals—Korea committed to exporting domestic unemployment.

[i] Complex nonresidency requirements aimed at tours of less than six months.

[j] Complex definitions.

[k] Some limitations designed to reduce excesses.

[l] Accompanied tour only. If family of head of household remains in Canada, all worldwide earnings are subject to full taxation.

[m] Recently liberalized policies in order to encourage acceptance of overseas assignments.

[n] Recently liberalized tax policies to encourage acceptance of overseas assignments.

[o] Some limitations.

SOURCE: Report of the Task Force to Study the Tax Treatment of Americans Working Overseas (Washington, D.C.: The President's Export Council, December 5, 1979), reprinted in U.S. Congress, Senate, Committee on Finance, Subcommittee on Taxation and Debt Management, *Hearings on Taxation of Foreign Earned Income*, 96th Congress, 2d session, June 26, 1980, p. 96.

TABLE 2

Examples of High- and Low-Tax Countries, Relative to the United States

Higher Than U.S. Tax	*Generally Higher Than U.S. Tax*	*Lower Than U.S. Tax*
Austria	Argentina[a]	Bahamas[j]
Barbados	Australia[b]	Belgium[k]
Canada	Brazil[b]	Bermuda[j]
Chile	Costa Rica[b]	Dominican Republic
Columbia	Germany[c]	El Salvador
Cyprus	Greece[b]	France
Denmark	Iran[d]	Guatemala
Ecuador	Italy[e]	Honduras
Ethiopia	Japan[c]	Hong Kong
Finland	Malawi[f]	Kuwait[j]
India	Mexico[g]	Lebanon
Indonesia	Morocco[h]	Mozambique
Ireland	Nigeria[b]	Netherlands
Jamaica	South Africa[i]	Nicaragua
Kenya		Panama[j]
Korea		Paraguay[j]
Luxembourg		Saudi Arabia[j]
Malaysia		United Kingdom
Netherlands Antilles		Uruguay
New Zealand		Venezuela
Norway		
Pakistan		
Peru		
Philippines		
Portugal		
Puerto Rico		
Singapore		

[a] Lower than the U.S. tax for incomes under $25,000.

[b] Lower than the U.S. tax for incomes under $10,000.

[c] Lower than the U.S. tax for incomes under $20,000.

[d] Higher than the U.S. tax for incomes of $25,000-40,000, but lower than the U.S. tax for other income levels.

[e] Lower than the U.S. tax for incomes above $60,000.

[f] Lower than the U.S. tax for incomes above $70,000.

[g] Lower than the U.S. tax for incomes up to $10,000 and over $40,000.

[h] Lower than the U.S. tax for incomes over $50,000.

[i] Lower than the U.S. tax for incomes of $15,000 or less.

[j] No income tax applicable.

[k] Higher than the U.S. tax for incomes over $80,000.

SOURCE: Marcia Field and Brian Gregg, "U.S. Taxation of Foreign Earned Income of Private Employees," in *Essays in International Taxation: 1976* (Washington, D.C.: Department of the Treasury, 1976), table 10, p. 127, derived by the Office of Tax Analysis from the Price-Waterhouse Information Guide, *Individual Income Taxes in 80 Countries,* January 1975.

credit would not fully offset U.S. taxes and countries whose taxes would fully offset U.S. taxes on the same income.

The foreign tax credit in U.S. tax law does not allow credit for consumption-type or value-added taxes used in a number of countries to reduce or eliminate reliance on income taxes. U.S. citizens working in these countries may pay large amounts in consumption-type taxes and still be obligated to pay at least the equivalent of the U.S. income tax rate on foreign-earned income.

Prior U.S. Law

The U.S. income tax was adopted in 1913. In 1926 Congress, on the initiative of the House Ways and Means Committee, voted to exclude from the tax an unlimited amount of foreign-earned income for individuals who resided outside the country for six months or more. The exclusion was referred to as the "foreign trader" exemption, for it was intended to benefit export salesmen, although the exclusion was not specifically limited to those engaged in export trade. The legislative history of this provision shows that Congress was concerned solely with providing an incentive for U.S. citizens to live overseas and it did not base its action on concern for the equity of the foreign trader tax exclusion.[5]

In 1932 Congress narrowed the exclusion to cover only persons in the private sector, consistent with the foreign trader purpose of its original enactment. In 1942 an attempt was made to repeal the exclusion, but instead the eligibility requirement was increased from more than six months' residence outside the United States to bona fide residence in a foreign country for an entire tax year. This change was made to eliminate abuses by those who deliberately absented themselves from the country for half a year to escape taxation.[6] In 1951 the exclusion was amended to provide eligibility other than through bona fide residence if the U.S. citizen was present in one or more foreign countries for 510 full days (seventeen months) out of eighteen consecutive months. The physical-presence provision was intended to encourage citizens to go abroad and to place them on an equal footing with citizens of other countries. Congress was particularly anxious to encourage managers, technicians, and skilled workers to go abroad for periods of eighteen to thirty-six months to complete specific projects. This encouragement was consistent with the objectives of the Point Four Program, and Congress recognized that many of these workers would be unable to meet the bona fide residence test.[7] Some citizens, such as movie personnel, took advantage of the physical-presence provision to perform work overseas that was customarily performed in this country. Congress, to counter such actions, amended the physical-presence provision in 1953 to limit the exclusion to $20,000 per taxable year.[8] In 1962 Congress limited those claiming exemption for foreign-earned income under the bona fide residence provision to $20,000 a year for the first three years and $35,000 a year thereafter. The higher exclusion after three years of residence abroad was provided in recognition that those who are abroad for long periods of time become more dependent on the foreign economy and less upon the U.S. economy.[9] In 1964 the $35,000 ceiling on the exclusion for bona fide residents was lowered to $25,000.

In 1976 the relevant congressional committees concluded that the foreign-earned income exclusion in section 911 of the Internal Revenue Code should be retained so the competitive position of U.S. firms abroad would not be jeopardized, but a number of changes were adopted by Congress in the name of tax equity, including the following. The exclusion was reduced to $15,000 ($20,000 for employees of tax-exempt organizations). Those persons claiming the exclusion were denied the benefit of the foreign tax credit regarding foreign taxes on the excluded income. The income remaining after the exclusion was to be taxable at the higher marginal tax rate that would have been applicable if no exclusion had been claimed, the so-called exclusion with progression or exclusion off the bottom. These changes would more than double the U.S. taxes of citizens working abroad, according to Treasury estimates.[10]

A related development involving interpretation of another section of the tax code added to the concern of U.S. citizens working abroad. Many of these workers had believed that section 119 of the Internal Revenue Code permitted their exclusion of the value of employer-furnished meals and lodging, even if such in-kind compensation was not expressly provided for the convenience of the employer. In 1976 the Tax Court held that the value of Japanese living quarters furnished by employers of U.S. citizens was includable in the citizens' income at the higher local market value rather than at the price of similar quarters in the United States. U.S. citizens working overseas could then see that the value of other items of in-kind compensation would also be included in their gross income. The Treasury Department made a comprehensive study of the probable fiscal impact of the 1976 amendments and of the Tax Court decisions and found that the 1976 amendments would raise $318 million additional revenue in 1977, rather than the $44 million previously estimated, and that the Tax Court decisions would burden overseas taxpayers with an additional $65 million in taxes for 1976, for a total increase of $383 million over prior tax reporting practice or for an average of $2,700 per tax return.[11] Congress was thereafter unable to agree on substantive changes in the tax law affecting foreign-earned income. It twice postponed the effective date of the 1976 amendments. In the election year of 1978, Congress supplanted the prior law by adopting the Foreign Earned Income Act.

Current Law

The 1978 law revised the conceptual framework of the law on taxation of foreign-earned income. It preserved a section 911 exclusion for foreign-earned income in the narrow circumstance of the U.S. citizen who is a bona fide resident of a foreign country for an entire taxable year or is present in a foreign country for 510 full days (seventeen months) out of a period of eighteen consecutive months and resides in a "camp" located in a hardship area. The hardship area must be one designated as a hardship post by the secretary of state where extraordinarily difficult living conditions prevail, notably, unhealthful conditions or excessive physical hardships. The camp must constitute substandard lodging provided by the employer for its convenience because the area is remote and satisfactory housing is not available on the open market. The camp must be located near the place where the U.S. citizen renders services, it must be furnished in a common area or enclave that is not available to the public, and it must accommodate ten or more employees. The exclusion cannot exceed $20,000 for the taxable year, and the amount of the exclusion is to be prorated depending on the number of days the U.S. citizen resides in the camp. The U.S. citizen cannot claim the tax credit regarding foreign taxes on income excluded under this provision. The camp is treated as part of the employer's business premises; so the taxpayer can exclude the value of the lodging and employer-provided meals under section 119 of the tax code if other requirements of that section are satisfied. Congress felt that construction workers and others qualifying for the Camp 911 exclusion should receive that exclusion so that the employer would be less likely to replace U.S. employees with foreign workers because of tax considerations.[12]

Most U.S. citizens working abroad do not qualify for the Camp 911 exclusion. These taxpayers are, however, entitled, under section 913 of the tax code, to an excess-foreign-living-cost deduction consisting of four elements: general cost of living, housing costs, education costs, and home-leave costs. This approach to the problems of overseas workers, involving the application of complicated legislative definitions and rules, was adopted by Congress on the principle of providing greater equity between citizens working abroad and those working at home.[13]

The general cost-of-living deduction is the amount by which the cost of living abroad exceeds the cost of living in the highest-cost metropolitan area of the United States, other than Alaska, and is tied to the income of a federal employee of the grade level of GS-14, step 1, regardless of the taxpayer's actual income. The housing deduction is the excess of the taxpayer's reasonable housing expenses abroad over his base housing amount (generally one-sixth of his net income). The education deduction is generally the reasonable schooling expenses of the taxpayer's dependents at the primary and secondary school levels. The deduction for annual home leave allows the reasonable cost of coach fare transportation from the taxpayer's work site abroad to his most recent place of residence within the United States. Some taxpayers living and working in certain hardship areas are allowed a special $5,000 deduction to compensate them for hardships and to encourage them to accept employment in these areas. A taxpayer cannot claim both the hardship post (Camp 911) exclusion and the $5,000 hardship deduction.[14]

U.S. Citizens Potentially Affected

President Carter's January 1980 report to Congress on tax treatment of U.S. citizens living abroad[15] concedes that there is no accurate count of how many citizens live overseas other than those who are civilian or military employees of the government. The State Department estimated that on June 1979 there were 1.5 million nongovernment individuals, including dependents, living abroad. This figure is derived from registration of U.S. citizens with U.S. consular offices overseas with adjustments based on estimates of those who fail to register. The 1970 census reported 236,000 citizens and dependents overseas other than government personnel. The president's report cautions that this figure may be conservative since reporting was voluntary and probably incomplete.

Tax returns filed for the 1976 tax year (not including returns filed from military post offices) show there were 174,000 U.S. citizens abroad (440,000 including dependents). Approximately 140,000 of these returns claimed the section 911 exclusion of foreign-earned income. The other 34,000 returns were presumably filed by those who would not remain abroad long enough to qualify for the exclusion or whose income consisted of investment income. Of course, some U.S. workers may not have filed returns, either because they did not earn enough or because they failed to report. Assuming that 140,000 U.S. citizens who are social-security recipients and who live abroad did not have taxable income, the president's report suggests there may be 600,000 nongovernment U.S. citizens, including dependents, who live abroad.

3

Principal Legislative Proposals

Recent recommendations for dealing with the taxation of foreign-earned income range from the complete exclusion of all foreign income (earned and unearned) attributable to activities while resident abroad for twelve months or more at one extreme to the repeal of all special exclusions and deductions at the other extreme.[16] The principal proposals now pending before the Congress are summarized in table 3. The administration's proposal, as this report is written, has been favorably reported by the Senate Finance Committee.

TABLE 3

PRINCIPAL LEGISLATIVE PROPOSALS—TAXATION OF U.S. CITIZENS LIVING ABROAD

Bill and Sponsor	*Foreign Residency Requirement (1)*	*Section 911 Income Exclusion (2)*	*Section 913 Deductions (3)*	*Foreign Tax Credit (4)*	*Other (5)*
Subtitle C of S. 394—Senator Russell Long (D-La.)	1. Bona fide residence for taxable year or 2. Physical presence abroad for 11 of 12 months. (Treasury secretary can waive requirements in case of civil unrest.)	Foreign-earned income while resident in developing country. Otherwise, excluded income must be from extractive or export-related services or from tax-exempt organization. $50,000 in income may be excluded, but bona fide resident for uninterrupted period of 2 years may exclude $65,000 for subsequent periods. May also exclude housing costs in excess of 16% of salary for GS-14, step 1.	May elect current deductions in lieu of exclusion.	Yes—but no credit allowed for foreign taxes on excluded income.	
S. 408—Senator John H. Chafee (R-R.I.) and 11 cosponsors	1. Bona fide residence for taxable year or 2. Physical presence abroad for 11 of 12 months.	Foreign-earned income not exceeding $50,000 plus ½ of the next $50,000 and housing costs in excess of 16% of salary for GS-14, step 1.	Section 913 would be repealed.	No change.	Camp lodging furnished by employer considered as furnished on employer's business premises for purposes of section 119.

S. 436—Senator Lloyd Bentsen (D-Tex.)	1. Bona fide residence for taxable year or 2. Physical presence abroad for 11 of 12 months.	Foreign-earned income not exceeding $75,000 in 1981 increased by $5,000 each year thereafter until maximum of $95,000 is reached in 1985.	Section 913 limited to housing allowance that may be taken in addition to the exclusion. Deduction covers reasonable expenses for one house for costs exceeding $5,500.	Yes—but no credit allowed for foreign taxes on excluded income.	Same as for S. 408.
S. 598—Senator Roger W. Jepsen (R-Iowa)	1. Bona fide residence for taxable year or 2. Physical presence abroad for 17 of 18 months.	All foreign-earned income.	Section 913 would be repealed.	Yes—but no credit allowed for foreign taxes on excluded income.	

(Table continues)

TABLE 3 (continued)

Bill and Sponsor	*Foreign Residency Requirement (1)*	*Section 911 Income Exclusion (2)*	*Section 913 Deductions (3)*	*Foreign Tax Credit (4)*	*Other (5)*
S. 867—Senator Daniel Patrick Moynihan (D-N.Y.)	1. Bona fide residence or 2. Physical presence abroad for 11 of 12 months. (Treasury secretary can waive requirement in case of war, civil unrest, or similar conditions.)	80% of foreign-earned income for personal services.	Section 913 would be repealed.	Yes—but no credit allowed for foreign taxes on excluded income.	

Section 302 of S. 969—Senator William V. Roth, Jr. (R-Del.) and 12 cosponsors	1. Bona fide residence for taxable year or 2. Physical presence abroad for 11 of 12 months.	Foreign-earned income from personal services not exceeding $50,000 plus ½ of the next $25,000 in income, and reasonable housing expenses for taxpayer and spouse and dependents living with him, in excess of 16% of salary for GS-14, step 1. Expenses of second home may be excluded if spouse and dependents do not live with taxpayer on account of dangerous, unhealthful, or other adverse living conditions.	Section 913 would be repealed.	Yes—but no credit allowed for foreign taxes on excluded income.	Same as for S. 408.
H.R. 911—Reps. Bill Archer (R-Tex.) and J. J. Pickle (D-Tex.) and 49 cosponsors	1. Bona fide residence for taxable year or 2. Physical presence abroad for 11 of 12 months.	Foreign-earned income not exceeding $75,000 in 1981 increased by $5,000 each year thereafter until maximum of $95,000 is reached in 1985.	Section 913 limited to housing allowance that may be taken in addition to exclusion unless taxpayer takes section 119 exclusion per column 5. Deduction covers reasonable expenses for one house for costs exceeding $5,500.	Yes—but no credit allowed for foreign taxes on excluded income.	Same as for S. 408.

(Table continues)

TABLE 3 (continued)

Bill and Sponsor	*Foreign Residency Requirement (1)*	*Section 911 Income Exclusion (2)*	*Section 913 Deductions (3)*	*Foreign Tax Credit (4)*	*Other (5)*
H.R. 913—Rep. Bill Frenzel (R-Minn.)	1. Bona fide residence for taxable year or 2. Physical presence abroad for 17 of 18 months.	All foreign-earned income.	Section 913 would be repealed.	Yes—but no credit allowed for foreign taxes on excluded income.	
H.R. 1317—Rep. Sam M. Gibbons (D-Fla.)	1. Bona fide residence for taxable year or 2. Physical presence abroad for 17 of 18 months.	Foreign-earned income not exceeding $75,000.	Section 913 would be repealed.	Yes—but no credit allowed for foreign taxes on excluded income.	

Administration's proposal. H.R. 3849—Reps. Barber B. Conable, Jr. (R-N.Y.) and Kent R. Hance (D-Tex.). Senate Finance Committee tax bill incorporating the administration's proposal is attached to H. Jt. Res. 266 as this is written.	1. Bona fide residence for entire taxable year or 2. Physical presence abroad for 11 of 12 months. (Treasury secretary can waive requirement in case of war, civil unrest, or similar adverse conditions.)	$50,000 in foreign-earned income plus ½ of the next $50,000, and reasonable housing expenses for taxpayer and spouse and dependents living with him in excess of 16% of salary for GS-14, step 1. Expenses of second home may be excluded if spouse and dependents do not live with taxpayer on account of dangerous, unhealthful, or other adverse living conditions.	Section 913 would be repealed.	Yes—but no credit for foreign taxes on excluded income.	Same as for S. 408.

(Table continues)

TABLE 3 (continued)

Bill and Sponsor	*Foreign Residency Requirement (1)*	*Section 911 Income Exclusion (2)*	*Section 913 Deductions (3)*	*Foreign Tax Credit (4)*	*Other (5)*
H.R. 1924—Rep. Richard T. Schulze (R-Pa.)	1. Bona fide residence for taxable year or 2. Physical presence abroad for 11 of 12 months.	All foreign-earned income.	Section 913 would be repealed.	Yes—but no credit allowed for foreign taxes on excluded income.	
H.R. 2014—Rep. William V. (Bill) Alexander (D-Ark.)	1. Bona fide residence for taxable year or 2. Physical presence abroad for 17 of 18 months. (Treasury secretary can waive requirement in case of civil unrest, war, or similar adverse conditions.)	All foreign-source earned and unearned income plus certain non-business income from U.S. sources.	Section 913 would be repealed.	Yes—but no credit allowed for foreign taxes on excluded income.	

H.R. 2113—Rep. Thomas J. Downey (D-N.Y.)	1. Bona fide residence for taxable year or 2. Physical presence abroad for 17 of 18 months.	$50,000 in foreign-earned income. Bona fide resident for 2 consecutive years may exclude $65,000 for subsequent periods.	Does not expressly repeal section 913.	Yes—but no credit allowed for foreign taxes on excluded income.	
H.R. 2172—Rep. Guy Vander Jagt (R-Mich.)	1. Bona fide residence for taxable year or 2. Physical presence abroad for 11 of 12 months.	Foreign-earned income not exceeding $75,000 in 1981, increased by $5,000 each year thereafter until maximum of $90,000 is reached in 1984.	Section 913 limited to housing allowance that may be taken in addition to exclusion unless taxpayer takes section 119 housing exclusion per column 5. Deduction covers reasonable expenses for one house for costs exceeding $5,500.	Yes—but no credit allowed for foreign taxes on excluded income.	Same as for S. 408.

(Table continues)

TABLE 3 (continued)

Bill and Sponsor	*Foreign Residency Requirement (1)*	*Section 911 Income Exclusion (2)*	*Section 913 Deductions (3)*	*Foreign Tax Credit (4)*	*Other (5)*
H.R. 3173—Rep. Les AuCoin (D-Oreg.)	1. Bona fide residence for taxable year or 2. Physical presence abroad for 11 of 12 months.	Foreign-earned income from personal services not exceeding \$50,000 plus ½ of the next \$50,000 in income, and reasonable housing expenses for taxpayer, and spouse and dependents living with him, in excess of 16% of salary for GS-14, step 1. Expenses of second home may be excluded if spouse and dependents do not live with taxpayer on account of dangerous, unhealthful, or other adverse living conditions.	Section 913 would be repealed.	Yes—but no credit allowed for foreign taxes on excluded income.	Same as for S. 408.

H.R. 4016—Reps. Sam M. Gibbons (D-Fla.) and Bill Frenzel (R-Minn.)	1. Bona fide residence for entire taxable year or 2. Physical presence abroad for 17 of 18 months or 3. Physical presence abroad for 11 of 12 months. (Treasury secretary can waive requirement in case of war, civil unrest, or similar adverse conditions.)	For those in categories 1 and 2 in column 2, all foreign-earned income attributable to personal service abroad. (If, however, individual is in top 10% in income of those qualifying for exclusions per column 2, and principal purpose of residence abroad is avoidance of U.S. income taxes, exclusion is subject to the ceiling set for those in category 3 of column 2.) For those in category 3 in column 2, foreign-earned income from personal services abroad not exceeding $75,000 in 1981 increased by $5,000 each year thereafter until maximum of $95,000 is reached in 1985.	Section 913 limited to housing allowance that may be taken in addition to exclusion. Deduction covers reasonable expenses for one house that exceed $5,500.	Yes—but no credit allowed for foreign taxes on excluded income.	Same as for S. 408.

SOURCE: Author.

4

Issues and Arguments

Effect on International Trade Objectives

The major theme of proponents of more favorable tax treatment for U.S. citizens residing abroad is that such treatment will help promote exports with concomitant benefits to the U.S. economy and employment generally. Critics of legislative proposals to provide more favorable tax treatment insist that the effect of such changes on exports and employment is overstated and the nation will be better served by a different policy.

Historical Purpose of Special Treatment of Foreign-Earned Income. Proponents of more favorable tax treatment of U.S. citizens residing abroad maintain that the exclusion of foreign-earned income from federal tax liability was adopted as congressional policy within a few years of the enactment of the federal income tax. Congress adopted the policy of complete exclusion with the single purpose of promoting export trade. Congress, in amending the statute in 1951, reiterated its purpose of encouraging citizens to go abroad, recognizing the added need at that time to encourage technicians to work abroad consistent with the objectives of the Point Four Program. Congress endorsed the 1951 amendments as placing our citizens who work abroad on an equal position with expatriate workers of other countries who are not taxed by their own countries.[17] Proponents note that even when other guiding principles led to the ill-fated 1976 amendments, Congress rejected the notion of completely ending the exclusion of income because it did not want to jeopardize the competitive position of U.S. firms abroad.[18] According to proponents, the original purpose of the exclusion of foreign-earned income is as important to international trade policy today as it was when the exclusion was first adopted in 1926, and Congress should again provide strong incentives for U.S. citizens to live and work abroad.

Opponents of more favorable tax treatment for U.S. citizens residing abroad contend that the historical purpose ignores the important policy principle of tax equity. Most of the pending legislative proposals would treat citizens residing abroad more favorably than they treat citizens living and working in the United States. The section on fairness in this analysis gives additional tax equity arguments. Opponents note that the 1926 statute was not limited to persons working in export-related activities; so the historical purpose relied on by proponents is served, by most bills for more favorable tax treatment, only in selected instances, if at all.[19]

Effect of Recent Increased Taxes on Employment and Export Sales. Surveys by the General Accounting Office show that the percentage of U.S. citizens in the expatriate work force of U.S. business activities abroad dropped between 1976, when a tax law much less favorable to such workers was adopted, and 1980 as follows: construction, including architectural and engineering work, from 65.1 percent to 44.7 percent; aerospace from 74.8 percent to 62.1 percent; resources extraction from 52.1 percent to 34.6 percent; and manufacturing from 60 percent to 56 percent. Overseas Resources Counselors, consultants to 306 corporate clients on overseas employment, reports a drop of 39 percent in overseas employment of U.S. citizens by its clients between 1979 and 1980. Chase Econometric Associates, Inc., reports that a higher percentage of U.S. workers overseas, in some cases as high as 50 percent or more, are returning to the United States.[20] The President's Export Council reported that recruiting firms in France, Germany, Italy, and the United Kingdom report that they are swamped with requests for qualified citizens to replace U.S. workers who are going back to the United States and that several leading U.S. contractors in the Middle East have reduced their U.S. staffs by more than 40 percent and have adopted hiring practices that specifically exclude U.S. citizens on future work.[21]

Proponents of more favorable tax treatment attribute the reduction in the U.S. labor force abroad to the less favorable tax treatment of U.S. citizens working abroad. The General Accounting Office found that nationals of other countries can usually avoid home country taxes by severing residency ties with the home country, but the United States taxes foreign-source income on a citizenship basis; so our workers are at a disadvantage in such competition. U.S. workers abroad are taxed by the United States and often their worldwide income is also fully taxed by the host country.[22]

According to advocates of more favorable tax treatment, the deductions provided by the 1978 law are clearly inadequate. The General Accounting Office cites survey results showing that U.S. workers overseas are being taxed on a significant part of their cost-of-living allowances—47 percent in the case of married individuals and 40 percent in the case of single individuals.[23]

Many firms employing U.S. citizens abroad reimburse these employees for certain extra costs of living abroad, frequently including the additional taxes they are required to pay, often amounting to 40 percent or more of the employee's base pay. In some cases those payments in effect double or triple the worker's salary. Tax reimbursement by U.S. companies constitutes a major proportion of the cost differential between employing U.S. citizens overseas and employing expatriates of other nations. A 1978 report by the General Accounting Office noted that over 90 percent of the 161 companies surveyed provided an educational allowance, over 80 percent provided cost-of-living, housing, and home-leave allowances, 77 percent reimbursed for additional taxes, almost 70 percent provided an overseas premium, and between 15 percent and 20 percent provided rest and recuperation allowances.[24] Firms electing to reimburse their U.S. employees overseas for taxes and other extraordinary living expenses find that this practice can lead to spiraling costs as the reimbursement adds to employees' income taxable by the United States and the host country and still more reimbursement is required each year to cover taxes on the augmented income. This compounding of earnings by the inclusion of tax and other reimbursements in income amounts to adding a tax on a tax and increases the employers' reimbursement liabilities substantially. One survey showed that firms reimbursing employees for taxes had to make tax equalization payments of $12,500 more per employee in 1979 than in 1976.[25]

A 1978 GAO study concluded, "A company that reimburses its American employees for higher taxes must either absorb the increased costs or pass them on to customers, thus becoming less competitive vis-à-vis other firms."[26] Chase Econometrics concluded from survey and other analyses that the cost of maintaining workers overseas has risen substantially because of the 1978 tax law changes and has added 2 percent to 10 percent to the cost of U.S. goods and services depending on the industry involved. It also concluded that the increased costs reduced the number of U.S. workers abroad, reduced the competitiveness of U.S. goods and services abroad, and resulted in a drop in exports of about 5 percent. Moreover, the loss of export markets has been principally in areas where markets are expanding and where the loss in market share will be felt long into the future.[27]

According to the General Accounting Office, a U.S. company's losing a contract to an overseas foreign competitor has a ripple effect, since other U.S. companies that would have provided services or materials for the performance of the contract lose that business. Increased taxes on Americans working abroad will affect export sales through higher prices, which will affect willingness to invest in export and overseas activities. The extent to which a firm replaces U.S. employees overseas with nationals of the host country or expatriates from other countries to cut costs and stay competitive may also have a ripple effect. Foreign employees are likely to deal with firms in their own countries for supplies and services needed in the performance of the contract.[28]

In sum, proponents of more favorable tax treatment of U.S. citizens working abroad maintain that, if employees must absorb increased tax costs of working abroad, they will return to the United States and our foreign sales will suffer or, if firms reimburse their employees for some or all of the extra expenses of working overseas, our firms will become less competitive. Companies will hire less expensive nationals from other countries to replace expensive U.S. workers, and, again, our foreign sales will decline. Commerce Secretary Malcolm Baldridge contends, "We are the only country in the world that shoots ourselves in the foot this way."[29]

Opponents of more favorable tax treatment of U.S. citizens working abroad deny that recent tax law changes have significantly hurt our export sales position. First they note that when the host country has income tax rates approximately as high as those in the United States, the foreign tax credit offsets the taxes paid by U.S. workers to the host country. They argue that our tax policy should cause no significant wage differential between U.S. and foreign workers hired in a host country whose taxes are as high or higher than U.S. taxes. They cite the large number of countries listed in table 2 to show that a majority of foreign countries in fact have tax rates equal to or higher than those of the United States. So far as the overall trend of employment of U.S. workers abroad is concerned, Jane G. Gravelle and Donald W. Kiefer of the Congressional Research Service contend that substitution of foreign workers for U.S. citizens overseas has been going on for years for other reasons.[30] Opponents cite President Carter's conclusion that studies undertaken on the taxation of U.S. workers living abroad do not provide clear evidence of competitive disadvantage to U.S. economic interests. Donald C. Lubick, assistant secretary of the treasury for tax policy in the Carter administration, maintained that, overall, the number of U.S. citizens living abroad seems to be increasing and our exports have been increasing at the rate of 25 percent a year. He saw no need for special incentives for Americans to work in Canada, Mexico, Japan, Western Europe, or Rio and said that factors other than the nationality of the purchasing agent were responsible for Americans' purchase of foreign autos in larger numbers.[31] Some opponents have contended that substitution of foreign nationals for U.S. employees may be good, because foreign nationals may constitute a more effective sales force than Americans. Such nationals, if citizens of the host country, will know the language better than U.S. citizens and may have greater rapport with the personnel with whom they are dealing.[32]

Some opponents maintain that changes in the level of taxation have little effect on the willingness of U.S. citizens to live overseas. In any event, according to Gravelle and Kiefer, the U.S. citizens employed abroad may not be selling U.S. products. They may engage in foreign production that, in fact, competes with U.S. exports and creates goods that may be sold as imports into the United States. Thus it cannot be said that reducing the number of employees so occupied reduces American exports.[33] According to these opponents, pursuing policies of tax equity and neutrality is more important than providing U.S. workers on foreign soil with advantages over U.S. workers at home. The section on fairness in this chapter contains additional discussion of these arguments.

Effect of Reducing Taxes on Employment and Export Sales. Proponents of more favorable tax treatment of U.S. workers abroad maintain that just as increasing taxes on these workers has increased their cost to business, which has, in turn, reduced their number with consequent loss in export sales, so reducing taxes would help U.S. firms become more competitive in the world market. The proponents note that, in addition to the surveys and experiences already cited, a study performed for the Treasury Department in 1978 by Professor John Mutti determined that high levels of U.S. exports are associated with the presence of U.S. citizens abroad and that these workers make an independent and statistically significant contribution to U.S. exports. A 1 percent decrease in U.S. citizens abroad is estimated to reduce U.S. exports by somewhat over one-half of 1 percent.[34] Proponents also cite the conclusion of the President's Export Council that U.S. citizens working abroad are essential to a viable export program. An increase in the number of citizens assigned abroad can increase our exports, reduce the negative balance of payments, enhance our country's image, and raise employment in the United States.[35] The Chase Econometrics study concluded that export losses from recent tax law changes were felt in emerging-market countries where such high-value-added U.S. exports as construction and engineering were reduced along with the substantial volume of merchandise exports generated by major projects. Chase Econometrics estimated that a 5 percent reduction in projected real exports in 1980 would reduce the value of exports by $16.2 billion and increase unemployment by 80,000 workers.[36] Thus it is hoped that changing tax policy to encourage U.S. citizens to work abroad will again capture major projects for U.S. firms.

Proponents of more favorable tax treatment insist that increased exports will increase gross national product and total employment for U.S. workers. The President's Export Council concluded that if the U.S. decided on policies that would increase exports by at least $30 billion annually as a means of bringing trade accounts into balance, at least 1.2 million new jobs would result.[37] Firms engaging in large-scale projects overseas find insufficient local labor for technical, skilled, management, clerical, and sales positions. More favorable tax treatment would help capture such projects and, consequently, would produce new jobs both for U.S. citizens overseas and, through export orders to supply these projects, for citizens at home. U.S. firms, in a very real sense, are selling the services of their employees. Foreign residents observe the consumption habits of U.S. citizens working abroad and attempt to emulate these habits, thus, it is claimed, stimulating additional demand for U.S. products.[38]

Proponents of the more favorable tax policy to encourage U.S. citizens to work overseas cite other benefits: showing the flag, bringing back ideas, and fostering international understanding and good will.[39]

Opponents of more favorable tax treatment of U.S. citizens working abroad claim that the relationship between U.S. tax treatment of citizens working in other countries, the quantity of U.S. exports, and overall employment is indirect and uncertain. Opponents criticize the studies of Mutti, Chase Econometrics, and the General Accounting Office, claiming that these studies overestimate the adverse employment and trade effects of the 1978 tax amendments and that the proposed tax changes may not appreciably increase exports. They cite the statement of the President's Export Council that most export activity takes place in the United States and conclude that measures to reduce domestic taxes or costs of production may be more effective and preferred by exporters.[40]

Opponents maintain that if taxes on U.S. citizens working abroad are cut, the firms that reimburse employees for such taxes will reap the benefit. The opponents find that more favorable tax treatment essentially provides a subsidy for businesses employing U.S. citizens overseas. This subsidy violates the principle of tax neutrality, which holds that tax policy should provide neither incentives nor disincentives for U.S. workers to work abroad. These opponents favor the policy of the 1978 law that allows deductions in order to adjust for differing living costs abroad because they feel it promotes neutrality while a flat across-the-board exclusion, as proposed in several bills, often provides a break unrelated to actual living costs. Gravelle and Kiefer contend that next to varying federal taxes for U.S. workers from foreign country to foreign country to achieve tax neutrality, the best approach to tax neutrality would be to repeal the exclusion and deductions now provided U.S. workers in sections 911 and 913. In this view, if the U.S. employee overseas feels he is not adequately compensated, we should let the market decide whether his wages should be raised or whether he has overvalued his services.[41] In sum, these opponents maintain that the principles of tax neutrality and equity are more important than stimulus to employment through a tax subsidy.

Gravelle and Kiefer maintain that improving the balance of trade is not a worthy objective of tax law changes for, with flexible exchange rates, an improvement in the balance will be minor and temporary. Market forces will adjust the balance automatically by increasing the price of the dollar, which will reduce U.S. exports and increase imports so that any temporary gain will be lost. If we wish to intervene in the foreign exchange market even on a short-term basis, we have more efficient ways to do so than by changing tax law.[42]

Proponents of more favorable tax treatment of U.S. citizens working abroad respond to opponents' arguments by claiming that direct measures to support exports are limited, but tax policy can and should be used to promote exports. Reginald H. Jones, chairman of the President's Export Council, stated in his December 19, 1979, letter transmitting the council's report to the president that tax law must enable U.S. citizens to face the uncertainties of life abroad so they can serve as the leading edge of the export growth necessary in today's world to maintain the economic role so essential to our welfare.[43] Some proponents argue, contrary to the tax neutrality approach of Gravelle and Kiefer, that we should not tax any foreign-earned income, just as many other leading trade nations encourage their citizens to serve abroad by not taxing their incomes. The United States is unique among the leading industrial nations in taxing on the basis of citizenship. The proponents argue that ours is a competitive world and, if we expect to hold our own in international trade, we should attempt to compete on equal terms and not let other nations have the benefit of major overseas contracts and sales.

Cost of Tax Policy Options

The tax revenue effects of various proposals for reform of taxation of the income of U.S. citizens working abroad are of particular interest to revenue officials and to opponents of more favorable tax treatment of such income. The U.S. budget for fiscal 1982 estimates tax expenditures for the deductions and exclusions permitted these taxpayers under the Foreign Earned Income Act of 1978 at $665 million.[44] One option available to Congress would be to return in principle to the 1926 law and allow an unlimited exclusion for foreign income of overseas workers. The bill S. 598, sponsored by Senator Roger W. Jepsen (R-Iowa), and H.R. 913, sponsored by Representative Bill Frenzel (R-Minn.), would retain the longer residency requirements of current law, repeal section 913 deductions, and provide an unlimited exclusion of foreign-earned income under section 911. The bills H.R. 1924, sponsored by Representative Richard T. Schultze (R-Pa.), and H.R. 2014, sponsored by Representative William V. (Bill) Alexander (D-Ark.), listed in table 3, agree with these provisions in most respects. The staff of the Joint Committee on Taxation places the revenue loss from the Jepsen bill at $610 million for calendar 1982.[45]

The administration's proposal, H.R. 3849, would also repeal section 913 deductions and provide an exclusion for foreign-earned income, but the exclusion would be limited to $50,000 plus half of the next $50,000 in earned income. Housing costs in excess of 16 percent of the salary of a government employee in grade GS-14, step one ($6,059), would also be allowed as an exclusion. The residence requirement for eligibility for these exclusions would be shortened to twelve months (or physical presence abroad for eleven out of the twelve months), which would make some additional persons eligible for the exclusions. The administration estimates this proposal will reduce tax collections by $500 million.[46] The staff of the Joint Committee on Taxation placed the revenue cost of a similar bill, S. 408 by Senator John H. Chafee (R-R.I.) and others, at $546 million for fiscal 1982.[47]

Proponents of more favorable tax treatment of U.S. citizens working abroad maintain that estimates of tax revenue losses provide only part of the picture. They note the General Accounting Office's finding that completion of tax returns under the provisions of the Foreign Earned Income Act of 1978 is so complicated that a high percentage of taxpayers rely on professionals to prepare their returns. Firms preparing individual tax returns for their employees estimated an average cost to the firms of $700 per return and, when professionals were hired from outside the firms, the cost was $1,100. If 112,000 taxpayers paid an average of $900 for professional assistance, compliance costs, even without the record-keeping costs required under the present complicated deduction system, would be more than $100 million. Proponents contend that much of this cost could be saved if the law were simplified as proposed in most of the pending legislative proposals.

These savings should be deducted from the $500 million revenue loss projected by the administration.

Proponents maintain that the more important objection to use of revenue loss figures is that they fail to take account of changes in behavior induced by tax law changes. In the proponents' view more favorable tax treatment of U.S. workers abroad will increase export sales, and additional taxes gained from increased business profits will more than offset the projected revenue losses. Chase Econometrics, in costing out the losses in federal tax receipts from the enactment of the 1978 legislation, calculated the dollar losses from a 5 percent reduction in U.S. real exports in 1980 at $6.5 billion, compared with the Treasury's estimate of increased tax revenues of $498 million. Proponents state that if their proposals stimulate as much gain in trade as Chase estimated was lost from the 1978 legislation, the cost-benefit equation is clearly favorable and the federal government will gain far more revenues than it will lose.[48]

Opponents of more favorable tax treatment for U.S. citizens living abroad contend that the relation between the tax changes proposed and the foreign-trade and business-income effects are tenuous, uncertain, and likely to be delayed. They view projections of increased tax revenues as overoptimistic. They feel the revenue loss projections are close to the mark and these losses would be sustained immediately, that is, for the first year for which the tax law changes are made effective. In the opponents' view, many taxpayers will continue to obtain professional assistance in completing their tax returns, particularly if their employers provide this assistance or fund it. The opponents conclude that the compliance-cost savings claimed are overstated.

Fairness

The fairness of alternative tax treatments for U.S. citizens residing abroad is subject to much dispute. The policy maker's judgment as to the fairest approach depends in substantial part on the principles of equity given the greatest prominence in the decision-making process.

General Principles. Opponents of more favorable tax treatment of U.S. citizens working abroad maintain that there are certain guiding principles of tax policy that should be followed as far as possible. These principles, they contend, are primarily ethical and subjective in nature. The two principles that are most relevant are tax neutrality and tax equity. Tax neutrality should be followed so that tax policy neither encourages nor discourages particular behavior, for example, service abroad. This neutrality permits normal economic forces and other considerations to control such decisions. Tax equity calls for a tax system that is fair both horizontally and vertically. Horizontal equity calls for taxing individuals in equal circumstances equally. The cost of living in some overseas posts is higher than in the United States. Living costs within the United States, however, vary considerably also. Present tax law does not define taxable income as that income which is net of living expenses. Thus it would offend the principle of horizontal equity, in the view of some opponents, to provide a deduction or exclusion to offset higher living costs in some posts overseas when no such deduction or exclusion is allowed for those in higher-cost locations in this country. A tax law provision that allows a deduction of $6,059 for a family in an overseas post, for example, and does not allow a similar deduction for a family in Boston, New York, Honolulu, or Anchorage is inconsistent with the standard of horizontal equity.[49]

Opponents point out, moreover, that a Treasury Department survey shows the majority of the tax breaks for overseas workers under the income exclusion effective in 1975 went to those in the wealthiest 15 percent of the population. Workers who are confronted with higher living costs in certain localities in this country demand correspondingly higher wages. Some opponents of more favorable tax treatment of overseas workers insist that U.S. citizens working in high-cost overseas posts should do as domestic workers do and bargain for higher wages to cover these costs rather than rely on special tax breaks that domestic workers do not enjoy. Special tax breaks that benefit primarily high-income overseas workers reduce the vertical equity of our tax system, and failure to provide equal breaks for domestic workers violates the principles of horizontal equity and tax neutrality.[50]

Proponents of more favorable tax treatment note that the current law, featuring special tax deductions for overseas workers, which was supposed to provide greater tax equity, fails to achieve tax equity among the workers living abroad, for example. These tax law provisions clearly favor married workers over those who are single. It is claimed that the tax benefits of section 913 deductions decrease as the worker's income decreases (deductions are more valuable to those with higher marginal tax rates), thus discriminating against low-income workers. Horizontal tax equity cannot be achieved even among resident taxpayers; and variations in the rates of host country taxes, costs of living from country to country, and so forth, make achievement of tax equity even more difficult when overseas and domestic workers are considered together.[51]

Proponents insist that, in view of the cited difficulties of achieving abstract principles of equity and the overriding need to promote international trade objectives, we should not blindly follow so-called tax equity principles. We should use international trade objectives as the primary touchstone in setting a suitable tax policy for overseas workers. The foreign trader exclusion adopted in tax law in 1926 did not rest on the policy of tax equity, but on the promotion of foreign trade objectives. The Senate Finance Committee reiterated this objective of government taxation of U.S. citizens abroad and added the objective of placing our workers overseas in equal positions with citizens from other countries who go abroad to work without being taxed by their native countries.[52]

In addition to citing special hardships involved in overseas service as justification for more favorable tax treatment, proponents contend that there is another principle of taxation that supports their view. Proponents contend a fundamental tenet of taxation is that the jurisdiction imposing a tax must earn its taxes by providing protection or services for the income-producing activities involved. Each government expends public funds to benefit primarily the residents of its own territory. U.S. citizens overseas do not benefit, it is claimed, from most expenditure of government funds in the United States. They receive no benefit from police protection in the United States or from Medicaid or Medicare. Rather, most host countries require that those U.S. citizens pay taxes to fund abroad some of the types of services that the United States funds domestically. Taxing U.S. citizens who are resident abroad simply cannot be justified on a quid pro quo basis.[53] Either nonresident U.S. citizens should not be taxed by the United States, or, if they are taxed by the United States, they should be taxed lightly.

Opponents respond that the tax benefits argument against taxing U.S. citizens working abroad assumes that all government expenditures are for the benefit of the individual when in fact these expenditures support collective goals, such as a strong defense, foreign relations efforts, and welfare activities, and some of these expenditures may be of substantial benefit to workers overseas. The government of the host country, for example, might find U.S. military assistance critical. In any event, opponents claim, the United States has not endorsed the tax benefits principle. It taxes income on the principle of ability to pay. The overseas worker receives some benefits from U.S. expenditures of tax revenues and from his citizenship, for a significant number of citizens have been unwilling to give up their U.S. citizenship even for the benefits of complete tax exemption.[54]

Fairness in Living Conditions and Expenses. Proponents of more favorable tax treatment of U.S. citizens living abroad contend that opponents' reliance on the principle of horizontal tax equity assumes that U.S. residents and U.S. citizens residing abroad are similarly situated in economic terms and have the same taxable income. Most U.S. citizens living abroad, however, have higher costs of living, and they may pay taxes to two national governments, thus substantially lowering their after-tax income. U.S. workers abroad often must use after-tax income to buy foreign substitutes for government and municipal services, such as Medicare and public education, which their U.S. taxes would buy if they were in the United States. Housing costs are notoriously higher in many locations abroad. Spouses and dependents frequently cannot obtain work permits in foreign countries to provide supplemental income as they could in the United States. Because of cultural differences there is a continuous mismatch of income and goods for U.S. citizens living overseas. Governments of some host countries tax the allowances that many firms provide in an attempt to offset some of the extra costs of living abroad, and this extra tax throws U.S. citizens abroad into higher and higher tax brackets without any increase in real income. U.S. taxation of income-tax reimbursement allowances and the amount by which other allowances exceed special deductions permitted under the 1978 statute, opponents claim, explains why many overseas workers are in higher U.S. tax brackets.

The inconveniences and hardships of living abroad often include unreliable or nonexistent public services, a hostile local population, and an unfavorable and unhealthful environment. U.S. citizens overseas, in addition, are totally disfranchised in the countries of their residence. Human life is cheap in many foreign countries, and U.S. workers may be subject to much higher risk of injury or death.[55]

There are additional reasons, according to proponents, why horizontal equity is not achieved by taxing U.S. residents and U.S. citizens overseas alike. When a U.S. citizen moves overseas, he forfeits some important advantages under U.S. tax law. Contributions to local churches, schools, and charities abroad are not tax deductible on U.S. tax returns; yet the same contributions made by residents in the United States are deductible. In the United States the taxpayer can deduct state and local sales taxes, including these taxes on large-ticket items such as automobiles, boats, and trailers. The U.S. citizen abroad has no such recourse. Not only may the U.S. citizen abroad not deduct consumption-type taxes on his U.S. tax return, but he faces much higher taxes of this type. The French, for example, raise more than 35 percent of their revenues from consumption-type taxes. Of the fifteen Organization for Economic Cooperation and Development countries, only Japan places less emphasis on value-added and other consumption-type taxes than the United States. Almost three-fifths of U.S. citizens residing abroad live in the other fourteen countries.[56]

Opponents respond that current tax law provides deductions to offset extra living costs abroad. The nondeductibility of contributions can be offset by routing contributions through U.S. charities. An extra $5,000 deduction is allowed on U.S. tax returns for U.S. citizens living abroad in hardship areas. Many overseas assignments involve neither hardship nor higher expenses. In the opponents' view the tax equity principle cited in the preceding subsection remains valid. Why, they inquire, provide special exemptions and deductions for overseas residents when we do not provide similar tax breaks for citizens who live in high-cost or hardship localities in this country? Medical expenses and casualty losses are allowed as deductions on U.S. tax returns because the resulting reduced ability to pay taxes is involuntary. Foreign employment with its concomitant expenses, however, is voluntarily accepted by the taxpayer. Thus the same principles of tax equity do not apply to these two categories of expenses. Horizontal equity requires that overseas workers not be given more favorable tax treatment than workers in the United States.[57]

Fairness of the Form of Relief Provided. Tax breaks for U.S. citizens working abroad generally take the form of tax credits, deductions, or exclusion of income. None of the pending proposals calls for repeal of the foreign tax credit. Assuming that some form of relief is allowed, the form of relief becomes quite important. Accordingly, this subsection discusses the arguments for and against income exclusions as compared with tax deductions. Current law relies primarily on deductions whose adequacy is the subject of dispute. Most of the reform proposals would rely only on exclusions, though a few proposals would combine a substantial exclusion with a single deduction, as for housing.

Deductions favored over exclusions. Those favoring deductions over exclusions maintain that an exclusion without an upper dollar or percentage limit would lead some citizens to reside abroad and perform the same functions they can perform quite as readily in the United States just to avoid paying U.S. income taxes.[58] An exclusion of a flat dollar amount is viewed by critics as unrelated to the living costs in most instances, a poor approximation of differences in living costs at best. If the taxpayer resides in a host country having low living costs and low income taxes, the taxpayer receives a windfall from the exclusion.[59] Thus, an exclusion of a flat dollar amount is viewed as arbitary and unfair.[60]

In contrast to exclusions, deductions can be fashioned to approximate closely the extra costs of living in certain overseas locations. These deductions need not overcompensate some taxpayers for excess living costs and undercompensate others. Thus they can come closer to providing tax equity and fairness in the tax system.

Exclusions favored over deductions. Those favoring income exclusions criticize the use of deductions because the U.S. tax deductions for excess living costs are, in their view, often inadequate and frequently less valuable than the $20,000 exclusion available prior to the 1978 law. The amount by which firms' allowances for excess living costs exceed the allowable deductions is taxable as additional income under U.S. law and the entire allowances may be taxable as additional income in the host country. U.S. workers abroad are thus thrown into higher income tax brackets, and the spiraling of income due to special allowances for taxes compounds the tax problems of U.S. workers overseas and increases costs to their employers. The General Accounting Office and others contend that the deductions provided in the 1978 statute fall short of providing adequate relief for overseas living costs. Taxes on the incomes of overseas workers are often far in excess of what they would have been had the workers remained employed in the United States.[61]

Another problem with the deductions provided in the 1978 law are their complexity and the substantial compliance costs they impose on U.S. workers abroad and their employers. Policing such deductions imposes high administrative costs on the Internal Revenue Service as well. In terms of tax equity, deductions are generally more valuable to those in higher income tax brackets who pay a higher marginal tax rate. Thus, such deductions add to the regressiveness of the tax system.[62]

Exclusions, on the other hand, are simple to use and police. Compliance costs are low. Because the effect of exclusions is readily understood, they are more likely to motivate workers to take overseas assignments, thus promoting international trade objectives. If an exclusion has a ceiling that does not fully cover the income of a significant percentage of overseas taxpayers, its benefits will favor lower-income workers over those in higher brackets, since the lower income will be fully excluded while the higher income will not. The income exclusion is also favored for employees of charitable organizations. These employees may not benefit from the foreign tax credit because the host country may not tax the incomes of charitable workers and, if this is true, U.S. charities may have to reimburse these employees for their U.S. income tax payments with money they would prefer to devote to the objects of their charity.[63]

Limited or worldwide coverage. The Carter administration announced support for a more liberal foreign-earned-income exclusion on August 28, 1980, as part of its Economic Program of the Eighties, but the exclusion proposal was to be limited geographically. Exclusion would be available to U.S. taxpayers in countries or areas where the Department of State authorizes a hardship allowance of 10 percent or more, thus including all countries of the Middle East. OECD countries and, for example, Bermuda, the Bahamas, Hong Kong, and Rio de Janeiro would not qualify as hardship locations. The Carter administration's 1982 budget cites this proposal as exempting the first $25,000 in income of U.S. nationals in hardship countries abroad and 60 percent of the next $60,000 for a maximum exemption of $61,000. This change was estimated to cost $320 million in fiscal 1982.[64]

The Senate Finance Committee voted, a week prior to the announcement of the Carter administration's proposal, to establish a $50,000 exclusion plus a separate housing exclusion for overseas workers in developing countries. This exclusion would also apply to U.S. citizens living in developed countries if they were engaged in charitable, export-related, or natural-resources activities, such as oil exploration. This proposal, part of a larger tax package, did not win congressional approval.[65] Section 121 of S. 394, introduced by Senator Long in the current Congress and outlined in table 3, provides the same pattern of coverage.

Limiting coverage, it is argued, targets tax benefits to U.S. citizens working in developing countries where a special incentive to work overseas may be required. Similarly, allowing an exclusion for income for workers in developed countries in particular activities will help promote those activities. Limiting coverage, however the choice of activities is made, reduces the overall cost of the income exclusion as compared with blanket coverage. Some critics insist that an exclusion will make work in some developed countries more attractive than work in the United States. Limiting coverage to help promote international trade objectives, for example, without providing any blanket incentive for U.S. workers to move to other developed countries, presumably would promote foreign trade in a more targeted manner than do most of the pending bills.

Critics of an exclusion for workers in export-related activities contend there may be a question as to the legality of such an exclusion as an export subsidy that would expose the United States to sanctions under international trade agreements.[66] Across-the-board coverage for the exclusion would presumably escape this objection. Critics also note that limited coverage would add complexities to the tax law and increase policing difficulties.

Notes to Text

[1] U.S. General Accounting Office (GAO), *American Employment Abroad Discouraged by U.S. Income Tax Laws* (Washington, D.C., 1981), p. 36. The test for citizens' of these countries achieving nonresident status and avoiding home-country income taxes on foreign-source income varies from country to country, but the GAO notes that a privately employed citizen would likely meet the test in the cited countries if he worked abroad continuously for more than two years, took his immediate family with him, gave up his home-country residence, and severed financial ties such as property ownership. See also GAO, *Impact on Trade of Changes in Taxation of U.S. Citizens Employed Overseas* (Washington, D.C., 1978), p. 6.

[2] GAO, *American Employment Abroad Discouraged by U.S. Income Tax Laws,* p. 17. The Philippines also taxes worldwide income on a citizenship basis, but that country is not a major trading nation. See *Martindale-Hubbell Law Directory* (Summit, N.J.: Martindale-Hubbell, Inc., 1981), Law Digest section, pp. 4085-86.

[3] 26 U.S.C. 901, 904.

[4] Some foreign countries whose expatriate workers are obligated to pay income taxes therein allow a foreign tax credit for income taxes paid in the country where the workers are employed to avoid double taxation. See GAO, *American Employment Abroad Discouraged by U.S. Income Tax Laws,* p. 36.

[5] House Report 1, 69th Congress, 1st session, p. 7; Brainard L. Patton, Jr., "U.S. Individual Income Tax Policy As It Applies to Americans Resident Overseas," *Duke Law Journal,* vol. 1975 (August 1975), pp. 691, 702; Charles M. Bruce, "New Regulations for Taxing Americans Living Abroad," *Taxes,* vol. 57 (February 1979), p. 79.

[6] Senate Report 1631, 77th Congress, 2d session, p. 54 (1942); Mel Levine, "Section 911: The Foreign Earned Income Exclusion—Death Blow or Recovery?" *Taxes,* vol. 56 (March 1978), pp. 169-71.

[7] Senate Report 981, 82d Congress, 1st session.

[8] Senate Report 685, 83d Congress, 1st session.

[9] Senate Report 1881, 87th Congress, 2d session. The president had recommended that U.S. citizens living in developed countries be denied an exclusion of foreign-earned income. A paragraph was added to the law providing that a U.S. citizen's representing to the authorities of a foreign country that he is not a resident of that country will be conclusive evidence that he is not a bona fide resident there for purposes of the tax exclusion under U.S. law. Thus the paragraph strikes at abuses by citizens seeking to avoid paying income taxes in either country. House Conference Report 2508, 87th Congress, 2d session.

[10] See Public Law 94-455; House Report 94-658, p. 201; Senate Report 94-938, Part 1, p. 210; Levine, "Section 911: The Foreign Earned Income Exclusion," pp. 173-76, discussing additional changes; Philip F. Postlewaite and Gregory E. Stern, "Innocents Abroad? The 1978 Foreign Earned Income Act and the Case for Its Repeal," *Virginia Law Review,* vol. 65 (October 1979), p. 1093.

[11] See John D. Maiers, "The Foreign Earned Income Exclusion: Reinventing the Wheel," *Tax Lawyer,* vol. 34 (Spring 1981), pp. 691, 698-701; GAO, *American Employment Abroad Discouraged by U.S. Income Tax Laws,* p. 2.

[12] See explanation of purpose in U.S. Congress, Joint Committee on Taxation, *General Explanation of the Foreign Earned Income Act of 1978* (Washington, D.C., 1979), p. 6.

[13] Ibid. For a more detailed explanation of these deductions, see Maiers, "The Foreign Earned Income Exclusion," pp. 704-10; *General Explanation of the Foreign Earned Income Act of 1978,* pp. 10-22; Anthony M. Komlyn and Peter W. Minges, "Foreign Earned Income Act Will Affect Americans Abroad," *Journal of Taxation,* vol. 50 (January 1979), pp. 38-42.

[14] See 26 U.S.C. 913. The statute also liberalizes the tax deduction for expenses for foreign-job-related moves by increasing the dollar limitations applicable to temporary living expenses. It extends up to four years, while the citizen is working abroad, the period for reinvestment of the proceeds realized from the sale of his principal residence. The statute was amended in 1980 to permit the Treasury Department, after consultation with the State Department, to waive foreign-residence or foreign-presence requirements cited in the text if the taxpayer must leave his foreign post before satisfying the residence or presence requirements because of extraordinary circumstances beyond his control. Civil unrest in Iran triggered adoption of this provision. See Public Law 96-608; Senate Report 96-1031, p. 5.

[15] Executive Office of the President, *Equitable Tax Treatment of United States Citizens Living Abroad* (Washington, D.C., January 24, 1980), attached to President Carter's letter to Congress of that date.

[16] See H.R. 2014 in table 3 for the exclusion of all foreign income (earned and unearned) and Postlewaite and Stern, "Innocents Abroad?" p. 1126, for the repeal of all special exclusions and deductions.

[17] Senate Report 981, 82d Congress, 1st session.

[18] Senate Report 94-938, Part 1.

[19] Compare Marcia Field and Brian Gregg, "U.S. Taxation of Foreign Earned Income of Private Employees," in *Essays in International Taxation: 1976* (Washington, D.C.: Department of the Treasury, 1976), p. 113.

[20] U.S. Congress, Senate, Committee on Finance, Subcommittee on Taxation and Debt Management, *Hearings on U.S. Taxation of American Citizens Employed Abroad,* 97th Congress, 1st session, April 24, 1981 (hereafter *1981 Senate Hearings on Taxation of Americans Employed Abroad*), statement of Frank C. Cona-

han, director, International Division of the General Accounting Office, p. 11; Robert D. Shriner, "Taxation of U.S. Workers Overseas Hurts Workers, Firms, and Exports," *Chase Econometrics U.S. Macroeconomic Forecasts and Analysis* (March 1981), pp. A-30, A-34, citing Overseas Resources Counselors data; *Economic Impact of Changing Taxation of U.S. Workers Overseas* (Washington, D.C.: Chase Econometric Associates, Inc., June 1980), executive summary, p. 2. A survey by the East Asia Mission of the Joint Economic Committee is cited to show that, in 1975, 19 percent of expatriate workers for a U.S. firm in Singapore were third-country expatriates, that is, citizens of neither the United States nor Singapore. By 1979, however, this proportion had increased to 41 percent and, because of the U.S. tax burden, Americans could not work as business representatives at the same level of compensation as expatriates from third countries. See Maiers, "The Foreign Earned Income Exclusion," p. 720. Representative Steven D. Symms (R-Idaho) testified that the U.S. engineering and construction industry's share of the Middle East market dropped more than 10 percent to less than 1.5 percent, and worldwide the United States has slipped in awards among competing nations from first in 1976 to seventh in March 1980 and from 16 percent market share to 4.9 percent.

[21] U.S. Congress, Senate, Committee on Finance, Subcommittee on Taxation and Debt Management, *Hearings on S. 2283, S. 2321, and S. 2418,* 96th Congress, 2d session, June 26, 1980 (hereafter *1980 Senate Hearings on Taxation of Foreign Earned Income*), p. 73; The President's Export Council, Subcommittee on Export Expansion, *Report of the Task Force to Study the Tax Treatment of Americans Working Abroad* (Washington, D.C., December 5, 1979), p. 3.

[22] *1981 Senate Hearings on Taxation of Americans Employed Abroad,* statement of Conahan, p. 9; GAO, *American Employment Abroad Discouraged by U.S. Income Tax Laws,* pp. 17-18; Maiers, "The Foreign Earned Income Exclusion," pp. 714-15; Patton, "U.S. Individual Tax Policy As It Applies to Americans Resident Overseas," p. 705.

[23] *1981 Senate Hearings on Taxation of Americans Employed Abroad,* statement of Conahan, p. 6.

[24] GAO, *American Employment Abroad Discouraged by U.S. Income Tax Laws,* pp. 18-23; GAO, *Impact on Trade of Changes in Taxation of U.S. Citizens Employed Overseas,* pp. 8, 30-31.

[25] Shriner, "Taxation of U.S. Workers Overseas Hurts Workers, Firms, and Exports," p. A-34. See Maiers, "The Foreign Earned Income Exclusion," p. 731, for an example of an almost doubling in three years of the reimbursement requirement for U.S. income taxes. The GAO provides an oversimplified illustration of continuing obligation to reimburse for foreign taxes based on one year of service abroad: reimbursement added nearly as much in Japanese taxes in three years as the amount of the first-year U.S. taxes. GAO, *Impact on Trade of Changes in Taxation of U.S. Citizens Employed Overseas,* p. 65.

[26] GAO, *Impact on Trade of Changes in Taxation of U.S. Citizens Employed Overseas,* p. 28.

[27] Chase Econometric Associates, *Economic Impact of Changing Taxation of U.S. Workers Overseas,* executive summary, pp. 1-2. The GAO notes that about 88 percent of the foreign affiliates of U.S. firms it surveyed held the opinion that the 1976 tax law changes would result in at least a 5 percent reduction in U.S. exports. GAO, *Impact on Trade of Changes in Taxation of U.S. Citizens Employed Overseas,* p. 10.

[28] GAO, *Impact on Trade of Changes in Taxation of U.S. Citizens Employed Overseas,* pp. 10, 13, 28.

[29] "Trade Policy: Baldrige Urges Measures to Improve Declining U.S. Export Outlook," *Bureau of National Affairs Daily Report for Executives* (hereafter *BNA DER*), May 18, 1981, p. L-1.

[30] Jane G. Gravelle and Donald W. Kiefer, *U.S. Taxation of Citizens Working in Other Countries: An Economic Analysis* (Washington, D.C.: Congressional Research Service, April 20, 1978), p. 57.

[31] President Jimmy Carter, Letter to Congress transmitting the report on *Equitable Tax Treatment of United States Citizens Living Abroad,* January 24, 1980; *1980 Senate Hearings on Taxation of Foreign Earned Income,* statement of Donald C. Lubick, assistant secretary of the treasury for tax policy, pp. 56-58.

[32] See, for example, Postlewaite and Stern, "Innocents Abroad?" p. 1124.

[33] Gravelle and Kiefer, *U.S. Taxation of Citizens Working in Other Countries,* pp. 48, 54. See Shriner, "Taxation of U.S. Workers Overseas Hurts Workers, Firms, and Exports," p. A-32, for the suggestion that certain Treasury employees feel that changes in the level of taxation would not affect taxpayer behavior.

[34] John Mutti, *The American Presence Abroad and U.S. Exports* (Washington, D.C.: Treasury Department, 1978), pp. 3, 21, cited in Maiers, "The Foreign Earned Income Exclusion," p. 721.

[35] The President's Export Council, *Report of the Task Force to Study the Tax Treatment of Americans Working Abroad,* p. 1.

[36] Chase Econometric Associates, *Economic Impact of Changing Taxation of U.S. Workers Overseas,* executive summary, p. 3; *1980 Senate Hearings on Taxation of Foreign Earned Income,* p. 147, exhibit 6 to report of Chase Econometrics.

[37] The President's Export Council, *Report of the Task Force to Study the Tax Treatment of Americans Working Abroad,* p. 4; Executive Office of the President, *Equitable Tax Treatment of United States Citizens Living Abroad,* p. 16; GAO, *Impact on Trade of Changes in Taxation of U.S. Citizens Employed Overseas,* p. 19.

[38] GAO, *Impact on Trade of Changes in Taxation of U.S. Citizens Employed Overseas,* pp. 12, 29.

[39] Maiers, "The Foreign Earned Income Exclusion," p. 729; Executive Office of the President, *Equitable Tax Treatment of United States Citizens Living Abroad,* p. 18.

[40] Gravelle and Kiefer, *U.S. Taxation of Citizens Working in Other Countries,* pp. 47-57; and see criticisms of studies cited in Maiers, "The Foreign Earned Income Exclusion," note 71, p. 702, and the statement of the locus of export activity in Executive Office of the President, *Equitable Tax Treatment of United States Citizens Living Abroad,* p. 22; Victor Thoronyi, "A Critique of the Chase Study of Tax Treatment of U.S. Workers Overseas, *Tax Notes,* June 30, 1980, p. 979.

[41] Gravelle and Kiefer, *U.S. Taxation of Citizens Working in Other Countries,* pp. 12-14, 22, 33, 48; Postlewaite and Stern, "Innocents Abroad?" pp. 1120, 1123.

[42] Gravelle and Kiefer, *U.S. Taxation of Citizens Working in Other Countries,* pp. 49-56.

[43] The President's Export Council, *Report of the Task Force to Study the Tax Treatment of Americans Working Overseas,* transmittal letter, p. 2.

[44] Executive Office of the President, *The Budget for Fiscal Year 1982* (Washington, D.C., 1981), p. 120.

[45] U.S. Congress, Joint Committee on Taxation Staff, *Description of Bills Relating to Tax Treatment of Foreign Earned Income,* Joint Committee Print JCS-11-81, April 24, 1981, p. 9. Calendar 1982 figures are cited since the Jepsen-Frenzel proposal would not be effective for a full year in fiscal 1982.

[46] "Treasury Department's General and Technical Explanation of H.R. 3849, Administration's Economic Recovery Tax Act of 1981," *BNA DER,* June 23, 1981, Special Supplement, p. 36.

[47] U.S. Congress, Joint Committee on Taxation Staff, *Description of Bills Relating to Tax Treatment of Foreign Earned Income,* pp. 7-8. Staff of the Joint Committee also estimated tax expenditures for the Bentsen bill, S. 436, at $615 million in fiscal 1982 and $727 million in fiscal 1985 when a higher exclusion ceiling would be in effect. The revenue cost of S. 867, sponsored by Senator Moynihan, was estimated at $520 million in fiscal 1982.

[48] See *1981 Senate Hearings on Taxation of Americans Employed Abroad,* statement of Conahan, pp. 8-9, on the cost of preparing tax returns; *1980 Senate Hearings on Taxation of Foreign Earned Income,* pp. 143-47, on the projections of Chase Econometrics as to the effect of the 1978 tax law changes. Chase counted another $1 billion lost because of the 1978 changes: $800 million in state and local tax receipts and $200,000 in unemployment-benefit payments.

[49] Gravelle and Kiefer, *U.S. Taxation of Citizens Working in Other Countries,* pp. 11-12, 39; Field and Gregg, "U.S. Taxation of Foreign Earned Income of Private Employees," pp. 111-12.

[50] Postlewaite and Stern, "Innocents Abroad?" pp. 1094, 1120; Gravelle and Kiefer, *U.S. Taxation of Citizens Working in Other Countries,* p. 33.

[51] Maiers, "The Foreign Earned Income Exclusion," pp. 691, 716-17, 726-27; GAO, *Impact on Trade of Changes in Taxation of U.S. Citizens Employed Overseas,* p. 33.

[52] Senate Report 981, 82d Congress, 1st session; Charles M. Bruce, "New Regulations for Taxing Americans Working Abroad," p. 79.

[53] Patton, "U.S. Individual Income Tax Policy As It Applies to Americans Resident Overseas," p. 699. Proponents note that the Senate Finance Committee recognized in principle the force of this argument in connection with its report on the 1962 amendments to section 911. The Committee based the establishment of a $35,000 ceiling on the foreign-earned income exclusion for those who had resided abroad for three consecutive years, compared with a $20,000 ceiling for those with between eighteen months and three years of residence abroad, on the recognition that those who are abroad for long periods of time become more dependent on the foreign economy and less dependent on the U.S. economy. Senate Report 1881, 87th Congress, 2d session.

[54] *1980 Senate Hearings on Taxation of Foreign Earned Income,* p. 55, statement of Lubick; Postlewaite and Stern, "Innocents Abroad?" p. 1121; Gravelle and Kiefer, *U.S. Taxation of Citizens Working in Other Countries,* pp. 43-44.

[55] Maiers, "The Foreign Earned Income Exclusion," pp. 726-28; GAO, *Impact on Trade of Changes in Taxation of U.S. Citizens Employed Overseas,* pp. 7-8, 76, 105-115; *1980 Senate Hearings on Taxation of Foreign Earned Income,* pp. 47-54, statement of the American Chamber of Commerce of Venezuela; and ibid., p. 547, statement of overseas housing costs furnished by Price, Waterhouse & Co.; Patton, "U.S. Individual Income Tax Policy As It Applies to Americans Resident Overseas," p. 693.

[56] Patton, "U.S. Individual Income Tax Policy As It Applies to Americans Resident Overseas," pp. 698, 705 (note 53), 913; Levine, "Section 911: The Foreign Earned Income Exclusion," p. 175; *1980 Senate Hearings on Taxation of Foreign Earned Income,* p. 415, prepared statement of Andrew P. Sundberg, director of American Citizens Abroad.

[57] See, for example, Field and Gregg, "U.S. Taxation of Foreign Earned Income of Private Employees," p. 112; Gravelle and Kiefer, *U.S. Taxation of Citizens Working in Other Countries,* p. 40.

[58] See, for example, Gravelle and Kiefer, *U.S. Taxation of Citizens Working in Other Countries,* p. 22; Senate Report 685, 83d Congress, 1st session. In 1953 a $20,000 limit was considered by the Senate Finance Committee sufficient to avoid the problem of deliberate residence abroad to avoid taxes.

[59] Thoronyi, "A Critique of the Chase Study," p. 981.

[60] Senate Report 95-746; Postlewaite and Stern, "Innocents Abroad?" pp. 1101, 1114.

[61] Maiers, "The Foreign Earned Income Exclusion," p. 726; *1980 Senate Hearings on Taxation of Foreign Earned Income,* pp. 279-83, statement of the American Chamber of Commerce in Hong Kong, and pp. 362-68, statement of Peter J. Hart, partner, Price, Waterhouse & Co., *1981 Senate Hearings on Taxation of Americans Employed Abroad,* statement of Conahan, pp. 2-8; GAO, *American Employment Abroad Discouraged by U.S. Income Tax Laws,* pp. 3, 8-15.

[62] GAO, *Impact on Trade of Changes in Taxation of U.S. Citizens Employed Overseas,* p. 79; Komlyn and Minges, "Foreign Earned Income Act Will Affect Americans Abroad," pp. 39-42; *1981 Senate Hearings on Taxation of Americans Employed Abroad,* statement of Conahan, pp. 8-9. See Postlewaite and Stern, "Innocents Abroad?" p. 1115, note 108, as to regressive nature of deductions.

[63] House Report 94-658, p. 201; and see Gravelle and Kiefer, *U.S. Taxation of Citizens Working in Other Countries,* p. 34.

[64] Executive Office of the President, *The Budget for Fiscal Year 1982,* p. 120; Maiers, "The Foreign Earned Income Exclusion," p. 725.

[65] Senate Report 96-940; Maiers, "The Foreign Earned Income Exclusion," p. 725.

[66] See Maiers, "The Foreign Earned Income Exclusion," p. 729.